The Art of Software Testing

First edition. April 16, 2025.

Written by Julian Cambridge.

The Art of Software Testing

To all the meticulous minds who tirelessly strive for quality and excellence in software, this book is dedicated. To the testers who question, challenge, and improve every line of code, your efforts pave the way for innovation and reliability. Your unwavering commitment inspires us all.

Introduction

In the rapidly evolving world of software development, testing plays a pivotal role in ensuring the quality, reliability, and success of software products. This book, "Navigating the Landscape of Software Testing," serves as your comprehensive guide to understanding and implementing effective testing strategies.

Test Activities and Tasks

Embarking on the testing journey begins with a clear understanding of the various activities and tasks involved. In this chapter, we delve into the specific tasks testers undertake during the software development lifecycle, including test planning, design, execution, and reporting. Through real-world examples and practical insights, we equip you with the foundational knowledge needed to collaborate effectively with development teams and stakeholders.

Test Types

Testing is not a one-size-fits-all process. Different test types offer unique insights into the software's functionality and performance. This chapter explores the diverse landscape of test types, such as functional, non-functional, regression, and acceptance testing. We'll guide you in selecting and implementing the appropriate test types to suit specific project goals and requirements.

Test Levels

Understanding test levels is crucial to structuring a comprehensive testing approach. From unit tests to system and integration tests, this chapter breaks down each level's objectives, benefits, and methodologies. You'll learn how to stack and execute these levels strategically to build a robust testing framework that minimises risks and maximises software quality.

Seven Testing Principles

Rooted in decades of industry experience, the seven testing principles offer invaluable wisdom for conducting effective tests. This chapter unpacks each principle—testing shows the presence of defects, exhaustive testing is impossible, early testing, defect clustering, the pesticide paradox, testing is context-dependent, and absence-of-errors fallacy—to guide you in creating thoughtful and efficient testing strategies.

Conclusion

By the end of this book, you'll possess a well-rounded understanding of the essential elements of software testing. Armed with this knowledge, you'll be better prepared to contribute to or lead testing efforts in your projects, ensuring that quality is ingrained in every line of code delivered. Whether you're a newcomer to software testing or seeking to deepen your expertise, "Navigating the Landscape of

Software Testing" is your key to mastering this critical aspect of software development.

Let's embark on this journey together and transform the way we perceive and implement software testing.

The Author

Julian Cambridge was born in London, UK.

- M.Sc. Business Computing
- B.Sc. (Hons) Computing with Business

Julian founded Golden Agile Solutions to supply IT consultancy activities to clients.

- Accredited Kanban Trainer (AKT, KMP, TKP)
- Certified Scrum Professional (CSM, CSPO, A-CSM, A-CSPO, CSP-SM)
- ICAgile Authorized Instructor (Agile Fundamentals, Agile Product Ownership, Agile Testing, Business Agility)

Table of Contents

Test Activities and Tasks

Test Planning

Test planning is a crucial phase in the software testing lifecycle. It involves defining the scope and approach for the testing activities, ensuring that all aspects of the software are adequately tested. Here's a high-level overview to get you started:

1. Objective Definition:

   - Clearly outline the objectives of the testing process. What are you aiming to achieve? This could involve verifying functionality, performance, security, or user experience.

2. Scope of Testing:

   - Determine which features and functionalities of the software will be tested. Define what is in-scope and what is not.

13

3. Test Strategy:

   - Develop a strategy that includes the testing levels (unit, integration, system, acceptance), types (functional, non-functional, regression), and the methods/tools to be used.

4. Resource Planning:

   - Identify the resources required for testing, including human resources (testers), hardware, software, and tools.

5. Environment Setup:

   - Plan and set up the test environments. This includes hardware, software, network configurations, and any other tools necessary for testing.

6. Scheduling:

   - Create a timeline for all testing activities. Include milestones for when different phases of testing should start and finish.

7. Risk Management:

  - Identify potential risks and obstacles in the testing process. Develop contingency plans to mitigate these risks.

8. Test Deliverables:

  - Define the documents and artifacts that will be produced during the testing process, such as test plans, test cases, test scripts, defect reports, and test summaries.

9. Entry and Exit Criteria:

  - Establish criteria that define when testing activities can start and when they can be considered complete.

10. Test Case Development:

  - Plan for the development of test cases and scripts based on the requirements and design documents.

11. Review and Approval:

   - Have the test plan reviewed by stakeholders to ensure it aligns with the overall project goals and constraints. Obtain necessary approvals.

12. Communication Plan:

   - Define how communication will occur among team members and stakeholders, including the frequency and type of updates.

Test planning lays the groundwork for a successful testing process, ensuring that the software meets its intended requirements and quality standards before release.

Test Analysis

Test Analysis is a critical phase in the software testing lifecycle where the testing team examines the requirements and develops a clear understanding of what needs to be tested. This phase lays the foundation for designing test cases and ensures that the testing process aligns with the project's goals and requirements.

Key Activities in Test Analysis

1. Requirements Review:

   - Analyse the project's requirements documents, user stories, and specifications to identify testable aspects. This ensures a comprehensive understanding of what the software should achieve and highlights any ambiguities or inconsistencies.

2. Identify Test Conditions:

 - Derive test conditions from the requirements. Test conditions are the aspects of the software that need to be tested, such as functionalities, performance, security, and other quality attributes.

3. Risk Analysis:

 - Perform a risk assessment to identify areas that may need more focus during testing. High-risk areas are those with complex functionality or where failure would have significant consequences.

4. Define Entry and Exit Criteria:

 - Establish the criteria for when testing activities should start and finish. Entry criteria might include the completion of requirement specifications, while exit criteria could involve achieving a certain level of test coverage or passing a percentage of test cases.

5. Prioritise Test Conditions:

 - Based on risk assessment and business priorities, rank the test conditions to focus on the most critical areas first, ensuring that testing efforts align with business needs.

6. Resource Planning:

 - Identify the tools, environments, and human resources needed for testing. This might involve selecting testing tools, setting up environments, and allocating team members based on their skills and availability.

7. Test Data Requirements:

 - Determine the data needed to support testing. This might involve identifying data sets, creating new data, or masking existing data to ensure privacy and compliance.

8. Define Test Objectives:

 - Clearly outline what each test aims to achieve, linking them back to the requirements and business objectives.

9. Collaborate with Stakeholders:

  - Engage with stakeholders, including developers, business analysts, and project managers, to clarify requirements and address any potential issues early on.

10. Documentation:

  - Document the test analysis process, including identified test conditions and risk assessments. This documentation serves as a reference for designing detailed test cases.

Test Analysis ensures that testing activities are structured, focused, and effective in uncovering defects that might compromise the software's quality. It's a proactive approach to managing quality and risk, helping to deliver a robust and reliable product.

Test Design

When we talk about test design, we're referring to the process of creating a plan to test something, usually a software or system, to ensure it meets the specified requirements and functions correctly. Here's a brief overview of the steps and concepts involved in test design:

1. Understanding Requirements: Before you design your tests, you need to have a clear understanding of what the system is supposed to do. This involves analysing requirements and specifications.

2. Identifying Test Scenarios: Based on the requirements, you identify different scenarios that need testing. These scenarios will cover successful operations, edge cases, failure scenarios, and more.

3. Designing Test Cases: For each scenario, design specific test cases. Each test case should include:

 - Test case ID

- Test description

- Pre-conditions (state of the system before test execution)

- Test steps (actions to be executed)

- Expected results (what you expect to happen)

- Post-conditions (state of the system after test execution)

4. Selecting Test Data: Determine the data needed to execute the tests. This includes input data, expected results, etc.

5. Creating Traceability Matrix: Sometimes it's helpful to map test cases back to requirements to ensure full coverage.

6. Prioritising Test Cases: Based on business impact, criticality, and risk, prioritise test cases to ensure the most important ones are executed first.

7. Setting up the Environment: Make sure you have the hardware, software, and network configurations needed to execute your test cases.

8. Review and Optimisation: Review the test design with stakeholders to ensure completeness, correctness, and efficiency. Make adjustments as needed.

9. Automation Considerations: Identify test cases that can be automated to save time and resources in the future.

These steps help ensure that your testing is thorough and that you catch any issues before they affect users.

Test Implementation

Test implementation involves putting your test design into action. It's about preparing everything necessary to execute the tests and encompasses several key activities. Here's how it generally unfolds:

1. Setting Up the Test Environment: Ensure the test environment is configured correctly. This includes hardware, software, network settings, and any tools needed for testing. The environment should mimic the production setup as closely as possible.

2. Preparing Test Data: Create or load the data you'll need for testing. This data should reflect real-world scenarios and include edge cases to fully validate the system's behaviour.

3. Test Script Development: If you're automating tests, write test scripts using your chosen automation tools. These scripts automate the execution of test cases, allowing for quicker and more reliable testing.

4. Tool Configuration and Integration: Set up and configure any testing tools you plan to use, such as test management, defect tracking, and continuous integration tools. Integrate these tools to streamline the testing process.

5. Test Case Execution: Execute the test cases as planned. This can involve running through manual test cases or executing automated test scripts. During this phase, you'll need to document any discrepancies between expected and actual outcomes.

6. Logging and Tracking Defects: As you discover issues, log them promptly in a defect tracking system. Include all relevant details such as steps to reproduce, severity, screenshots, and expected vs. actual results.

7. Regression Testing: After fixing issues, perform regression testing to ensure fixes haven't adversely affected other parts of the system.

8. Monitoring and Reporting: Continuously monitor the test execution process and track the status. Create test execution reports to communicate progress to stakeholders, including pass/fail rates and any blocking issues.

9. Feedback Loop: Implement a mechanism for collecting feedback on the test process and outcomes. Use this feedback to make improvements in future test cycles.

10. Final Validation: Before moving to production, conduct a final round of testing to ensure everything is functioning as expected. This may include a full regression test suite or a focused round of sanity tests.

By following these steps, you can effectively implement your test design, ensuring that your system is robust, reliable, and meets all specified requirements.

Test Execution

Test execution is the phase where the actual testing of the application occurs. Here's an overview of what happens during this phase:

1. Executing Test Cases: Run the pre-defined test cases either manually or using automated scripts. Ensure that each test case is executed as per the specified conditions.

2. Recording Results: Document the outcome of each test case. Indicate whether the test has passed, failed, or is blocked. Detailed notes on the execution are crucial for further analysis and debugging.

3. Logging Defects: When a test case fails, log a defect immediately. Provide detailed information about the issue, including the steps to reproduce, severity, screenshots, and any other relevant data.

4. Re-testing: After defects are fixed, re-execute the failed test cases to ensure the issues have been resolved.

5. Regression Testing: Perform regression tests on regions of the application that may have been affected by recent changes or bug fixes. This ensures that new code hasn't inadvertently broken existing functionality.

6. Continuous Integration: In environments with continuous integration, automated tests are executed regularly (often as part of the build process) to catch issues rapidly.

7. Monitoring and Reporting: Keep a close eye on the progress of test execution and periodically report status to stakeholders. This includes the number of test cases executed, passed, failed, and blocked, along with any critical defects.

8. Bug Validation: Once defects are fixed, validate the fixes by running specific tests to ensure the defects are properly addressed.

9. Adapting to Change: Test execution may uncover the need for additional tests or modifications to existing test plans. Continuously adapt and improve test cases and documentation as necessary.

10. Communication: Maintain clear and timely communication with the development team, stakeholders, and other relevant parties about test execution results and any issues encountered.

By diligently executing test cases and handling defects, you ensure that the software meets the required quality standards and is fit for release.

Test Monitoring and Control

Test Monitoring and Control is an ongoing process in the software testing lifecycle. It involves tracking the progress of testing activities and making adjustments as necessary to ensure that the testing objectives are met. Here's a breakdown of the process:

Test Monitoring

1. Progress Tracking:

   - Measure the progress of test execution using metrics such as the number of test cases executed, passed, failed, blocked, etc.

2. Status Reporting:

   - Regularly create and present status reports highlighting the current state of testing, any defects discovered, and the progress towards meeting the testing objectives.

3. Metric Analysis:

  - Analyse key metrics such as defect density, test coverage, and pass/fail rates to assess the effectiveness and efficiency of the testing process.

4. Quality Assessment:

  - Evaluate the quality of the product by assessing the severity and nature of defects found. This can help in making informed decisions about the readiness of the product for release.

5. Coverage Monitoring:

  - Continuously monitor test coverage to ensure all critical areas of the application are tested. Adjust focus to areas with less coverage if necessary.

Test Control

1. Issue Management:

   - Identify, log, and track issues as they arise. Work with the development team to prioritise and address these issues promptly.

2. Schedule Adjustments:

   - Modify the testing schedule to accommodate any deviations from the plan. This could involve reallocating resources, rescheduling test phases, or extending testing timelines.

3. Risk Mitigation:

   - Continuously assess and manage risks that arise during testing. Implement mitigation strategies to minimise potential impacts on testing objectives.

4. Resource Management:

   - Ensure that resources (human, technical, and environmental) are being used efficiently. Reallocate resources if necessary to address bottlenecks or prioritise critical testing activities.

5. Test Case Updates:

  - Modify test cases as necessary based on changes in requirements or the discovery of defects. Ensure that modifications are clearly documented and communicated to the testing team.

6. Communication and Collaboration:

  - Foster open communication among team members and stakeholders to ensure alignment on goals, progress, and any issues that arise.

By effectively monitoring and controlling the test process, teams can ensure that the testing objectives are met, quality standards are upheld, and potential risks are managed.

Test Completion

Test Completion is the final phase in the software testing lifecycle. It involves wrapping up the testing activities, ensuring that all objectives have been met, and preparing for project closure. Here's what this phase typically includes:

Key Activities in Test Completion

1. Ensure Coverage and Requirement Satisfaction:

   - Review and verify that all planned test cases have been executed and that they cover all the required functionalities. Ensure that all the requirements have been met.

2. Defect Closure:

   - Confirm that all identified defects have been addressed. Verify that critical defects are fixed and others are documented with appropriate justifications if not fixed.

3. Test Metrics and Reporting:

   - Compile test metrics and prepare a final report summarising testing activities, results, defect status, test coverage, and any quality improvements noted.

4. Test Summary Report:

   - Create a test summary report that includes an overview of the testing process, scope, objectives, outcomes, and any deviations from the plan. Provide an assessment of the quality of the product.

5. Lessons Learned and Retrospective:

   - Conduct a retrospective session with the team to discuss what went well, what didn't, and areas of improvement for future projects. Document lessons learned.

6. Documentation and Archiving:

   - Organise and store all test artifacts such as test cases, scripts, defect logs, and reports in a centralised repository for future reference.

7. Stakeholder Communication:

   - Communicate with stakeholders to provide clarity on testing outcomes, quality status, and any residual risks that may need to be addressed post-release.

8. Release Readiness Evaluation:

   - Assess the readiness for release. Make a recommendation based on test results, defect status, and risk assessment.

9. Resource and Environment Release:

   - Release resources (both human and technical) and testing environments if they are no longer needed. Ensure all accounts, tools, and environments are properly closed out.

10. Celebrate Success:

   - Acknowledge the efforts of the testing team and celebrate the completion of the testing phase. This helps in strengthening team morale and motivation.

Chapter 1: Test Activities and Tasks

Test Completion is crucial for ensuring that the product is ready for release with confidence, providing transparency to stakeholders, and laying the groundwork for future project cycles.

Test Types

Functional Testing

Functional testing is a type of software testing that validates the software system against the functional requirements/specifications. The purpose of functional testing is to ensure that the application behaves as expected and all functionalities work correctly according to the specified requirements.

Key Aspects of Functional Testing:

1. Test Scenarios: Identify and outline the test scenarios to cover all the functional requirements. These scenarios ensure that every feature of the application is tested.

2. Test Cases: Create detailed test cases derived from the test scenarios. Each test case should define the input, execution conditions, and expected results.

3. Inputs and Outputs: Use valid input data to test if the application behaves as expected. Also, include tests with invalid inputs to see how the application handles errors.

4. User Interface Testing: Verify that all user interface elements are functioning correctly, such as buttons, menus, and links.

5. Testing Types:

  - Smoke Testing: A high-level testing process to ensure that the most important functions work.

  - Sanity Testing: A narrow testing process that focuses on one or a few areas to verify a specific function after changes.

  - Regression Testing: Testing the complete application to ensure that recent changes haven't introduced new bugs.

6. Test Execution: Carry out the test cases manually or with automation tools. Ensure meticulous execution and record the results accurately.

7. Defect Logging and Tracking: When defects are found, they must be documented clearly with details such as steps to reproduce, severity, screenshots, etc., and tracked until resolved.

8. Re-testing and Validation: After defect fixes, perform re-testing to confirm that issues have been resolved and validate the software once all tests pass.

9. Reporting: Provide comprehensive reports that showcase the results of functional testing, highlighting any defects and areas tested.

10. User Acceptance Testing (UAT): Conducted with the end-users to ensure that the system meets their needs and expectations.

Functional testing is mainly concerned with validating if the functions of the software application are working as per the requirement specification. It is more concerned with the end result of the application rather than the internal processes.

Non-Functional Testing

Non-functional testing refers to the aspect of software testing that focuses on the non-functional requirements of a software application, which are the criteria not related to specific behaviours or functions. It is essentially about checking how well the system performs under certain conditions rather than what it does. This type of testing is crucial for ensuring the software's usability, reliability, and efficiency.

Key Aspects of Non-Functional Testing:

1. Performance Testing: Evaluates how the application performs under a specific workload. It includes:

  - Load Testing: Determines the system's behaviour under expected load conditions.

  - Stress Testing: Tests the system's behaviour under extreme conditions or peak loads.

- Scalability Testing: Assesses the application's ability to scale up or down based on demand.

- Endurance Testing: Evaluates the application's performance under sustained use.

2. Usability Testing: Assesses the application's user interface (UI) and user experience (UX). It ensures that the system is user-friendly, intuitive, and easy to navigate.

3. Security Testing: Identifies vulnerabilities, threats, and risks in the software and ensures data protection. It includes testing for:

- Data encryption

- Authentication and authorisation

- Network security

- Vulnerability assessments

4. Compatibility Testing: Ensures the software works on different devices, browsers, and operating systems. This includes:

- Browser compatibility

- Device compatibility (mobile, tablet, etc.)

- Operating system compatibility

5. Reliability Testing: Evaluates the software's ability to perform consistently without failure under certain conditions for a specific period.

6. Localisation Testing: Checks if the application is adapted for different languages and regions, ensuring content is culturally appropriate.

7. Accessibility Testing: Ensures that the software is usable by people with disabilities, adhering to accessibility standards like WCAG (Web Content Accessibility Guidelines).

8. Maintainability Testing: Assesses how easily the software can be modified to correct defects, accommodate new features, or be adapted to a changed environment.

9. Compliance Testing: Ensures the application's adherence to relevant laws, regulations, and guidelines to avoid legal issues.

Non-functional testing is essential for delivering a high-quality application that meets user expectations beyond just functional correctness.

Black Box Testing

Black box testing is a method of software testing that examines the functionality of an application without peering into its internal structures or workings. This type of testing focuses on the input and output of the software system, ignoring the inner code logic, structure, or overall program architecture. Here's a concise overview:

Key Characteristics

- External Perspective: It analyses software from an end-user perspective.

- No Knowledge of Internal Code: Testers don't require knowledge of programming languages or the software's internal logic.

- Focus on Outputs: Concentrates on the outcomes of specific inputs and the functional requirements of the application.

Types of Black Box Testing

- Functional Testing: Verifies that the software functions according to specified requirements.

- Non-Functional Testing: Assesses things like performance, usability, reliability, etc.

- Regression Testing: Ensures that new code changes don't adversely affect existing functionalities.

Advantages

- User-Oriented: Ensures the software meets user needs and works as expected.

- Highly Efficient: Detects discrepancies between actual output and expected results quickly.

- Broad Applicability: Suitable for various testing levels, such as unit, integration, system, and acceptance testing.

Disadvantages

- Limited Scope: Misses internal code-level bugs or optimisation issues.

- Possibility of Redundancy: Without insight into the code, testing may not always be optimised.

- Boundary Issues: Hard to design test cases for complex applications without some knowledge of the internal structure.

Examples of Black Box Testing Techniques

- Equivalence Partitioning: Divides input data into equivalent partitions to reduce test case numbers.

- Boundary Value Analysis: Focuses on testing at the boundaries between partitions.

- Decision Table Testing: Utilises tables to represent combinations of inputs and their expected outputs.

- State Transition Testing: Examines differences in outputs for varied input states.

Conclusion

Black box testing is indispensable for validating application functionalities and user interactions. It's particularly effective in catching issues that might only become apparent during real-world application use, ensuring that software delivers seamless user experiences.

White Box Testing

White box testing, also known as clear box or glass box testing, is a method of testing software that involves looking into the internal structures, logic, and workings of the application. Here's a breakdown of what white box testing entails:

Key Characteristics

- Internal Analysis: Testers have full visibility of the code and internal logic.

- Knowledge Required: Requires understanding of programming and system architecture.

- Focus on Code: Targets the code's internal structures, verifying logic paths, loops, and conditions.

Types of White Box Testing

- Unit Testing: Focuses on individual components or pieces of code to ensure they function correctly in isolation.

- Integration Testing: Verifies that different components or systems work together as intended.

- Code Coverage Analysis: Check extent of code executed, using metrics like statement, branch, or path coverage.

Advantages

- Comprehensive Coverage: Provides insight into internal structures, allowing for thorough evaluation and debugging.

- Code Optimisation: Helps identify areas for improving efficiency and performance within the code.

- Early Bug Detection: Finds and fixes bugs at an early stage, reducing potential impact on later development stages.

Disadvantages

- Complexity: Requires comprehensive knowledge of coding and can be time-consuming and complex to conduct.

- Less User-Centric: Focusing on code might overlook user experience and interface issues.

- Maintenance: Testing scripts must be updated with changes in the codebase, contributing to maintenance overhead.

Examples of White Box Testing Techniques

- Control Flow Testing: Analyses the flow of control through the program to find improper behaviours.

- Data Flow Testing: Examines the lifecycle of data within the program from creation to usage.

- Branch Testing: Ensures each possible branch in the program is executed at least once.

- Path Testing: Focuses on executing all possible paths through the code.

Conclusion

White box testing provides a powerful way to ensure the robustness and quality of software by delving into its internal workings. It complements black box testing by addressing different facets of software reliability and functionality, making it a critical part of a thorough testing strategy.

Test Levels

Component Testing

Component testing, also known as module or program testing, is a method of testing individual components of a software application. Here's an overview of what component testing involves:

Key Characteristics

- Focus on Individual Units: Tests are applied to specific components or modules rather than entire systems.

- Isolation: Components are tested in isolation from the rest of the application to ensure their correctness.

- Controlled Environment: Often utilises test stubs or drivers to mimic interactions with other components.

Objectives

- Verification of Functionality: Ensures that each component behaves as expected and meets specified requirements.

- Identification of Defects: Finds bugs and issues within the individual components.

- Validation Before Integration: Verifies the correctness of components before they are integrated into a larger system.

Techniques Used

- Black Box Testing: Testing component inputs and outputs without considering internal structure.

- White Box Testing: Examining the internal working of the component.

- Gray Box Testing: A combination of both black box and white box techniques.

Tools & Approaches

- Automated Testing Tools: Tools like JUnit for Java, NUnit for .NET help automate component testing.

- Manual Testing: Involves creating test cases and scenarios manually.

- Mocking and Stubbing: Use of mock objects and stubs to simulate interactions with other components.

Advantages

- Early Defect Detection: Finds defects at an early stage, reducing the cost and complexity of fixing them later.

- Focused Testing: Allows detailed examination of each component's functionality.

- Improved Quality: Contributes to higher quality and more reliable components before integration.

Disadvantages

- Complex Setup: May require complex stubs and drivers to simulate interactions with other system parts.

- Limited Scope: Primarily focused on individual components, possibly missing issues arising in integrated environments.

Conclusion

Component testing is an essential part of the software development process. By ensuring each part of the application functions correctly, it lays a solid foundation for further development stages like integration and system testing. Through careful implementation, component testing contributes significantly to the overall quality and reliability of a software product.

Component Integration Testing

Component Integration Testing is a level of the software testing process where individual software modules are combined and tested as a group. This type of testing is crucial for ensuring that integrated components work together correctly. Here's a detailed overview:

Key Characteristics

- Integration of Modules: Involves combining individual components or modules and testing their interactions.

- Focus on Interfaces: Concentrates on the interfaces and data flow between integrated parts.

- Sequential Approach: Typically follows component testing in the testing lifecycle.

Objectives

- Verify Interactions: Ensures that interfaces between components work properly.

- Detect Integration Issues: Identifies problems that occur when multiple components are combined.

- Validation of Data Flow: Checks that data is correctly passed from one module to another.

Techniques Used

- Big-Bang Integration: All components are integrated simultaneously, and testing is conducted on the complete system.

- Incremental Integration: Components are integrated and tested step by step, including:

  - Top-Down Integration: Starts from the top of the module hierarchy.

  - Bottom-Up Integration: Begins with lower-level components.

  - Sandwich: Combines both top-down and bottom-up approaches.

Tools & Approaches

- Continuous Integration Tools: Tools like Jenkins or Bamboo facilitate automated integration and testing.

- Pipeline Testing: Automated pipelines ensure regular integration and testing builds.

- API Testing Tools: Tools like Postman for testing interfaced components.

Advantages

- Early Detection of Systemic Issues: Identifies issues in the interaction to prevent more significant problems in system-level testing.

- Reduced Risk: Helps catch integration-specific defects early on.

- Facilitates Smooth System Testing: Lays down a reliable foundation for system and acceptance testing.

Disadvantages

- Complexity in Managing Dependencies: Handling dependencies between components may be tricky.

- Requires Detailed Planning: Needs meticulous planning to manage integration sequences adequately.

- Time-Consuming: Incremental approaches require time and resources, especially for larger systems.

Conclusion

Component Integration Testing plays a vital role in ensuring a seamless collaboration between various software modules. By identifying issues early in the integration phase, it reduces risks and contributes to smoother system testing phases. A well-planned integration testing strategy is essential to maintain software quality and reliability.

System Testing

System testing is a critical phase in the software testing lifecycle where a complete and integrated software system is examined to verify that it meets the specified requirements. It comes after integration testing and before acceptance testing.

Key Characteristics

- End-to-End Testing: Evaluates the entire system as a whole rather than individual components.

- Validates Requirements: Confirms that the system fulfils functional and non-functional requirements.

- Environment Simulation: Conducted in an environment that closely resembles the production environment.

Objectives

- Ensure Functionality: Checks if the software behaves as expected under various conditions.

- Performance Evaluation: Assesses system performance metrics like speed, scalability, and responsiveness.

- Reliability and Security: Tests the system's reliability and security features.

Activities and Types

- Functional Testing: Verifies each function operates in conformance with the requirement specifications.

- Performance Testing: Assesses the system's behaviour under different loads.

- Usability Testing: Examines the user interface and ease of use.

- Security Testing: Evaluates the system's protection against unauthorised access and vulnerabilities.

- Compatibility Testing: Ensures compatibility with different environments, such as browsers, devices, operating systems.

Tools Used

- Automation Tools: Tools like Selenium, QTP, or TestComplete for automating test cases.

- Performance Testing Tools: Tools like JMeter or LoadRunner to assess system performance.

- Security Testing Tools: Tools like OWASP ZAP for security evaluations.

Advantages

- Comprehensive Validation: Offers a complete validation of the software system, ensuring alignment with business expectations.

- Error Identification: Identifies defects that may not be apparent during unit or integration testing.

- User Perspective: Considers the overall user experience and operational environment.

Disadvantages

- Resource Intensive: Requires significant time, effort, and resources, particularly for large systems.

- Complex to Manage: Can be complex, especially when dealing with extensive and multifaceted systems.

- Difficult to Isolate Issues: Problems identified may be difficult to trace back to specific modules or components.

Conclusion

System testing is an essential process to ensure that the full software product is ready for deployment. It provides a comprehensive check to ascertain that the system functions as intended and can handle real-world scenarios post-launch.

System testing not only validates the functional aspects but also addresses performance, security, and user experience, making it a vital process for delivering a high-quality software product.

System Integration Testing

System integration testing is an important phase in the software development lifecycle. It involves testing the interactions and integration between different modules or components of a system to ensure they work together as intended. Here's a concise overview:

Purpose

- Verify Interface Accuracy: Check the interactions between integrated components to ensure they communicate and function correctly.

- Identify Issues Early: Detect interface defects and data flow problems before the system deployment phase.

- Ensure Compatibility: Confirm that combined parts deliver the overall expected system behaviour.

Key Activities

1. Planning: Design test cases based on interface design and interaction specifications.

2. Environment Setup: Create a suitable environment for simulating real-world interactions.

3. Integration Approach:

   - Big Bang: Integrate all components at once and test as a whole.

   - Top-Down: Integrate from top modules to bottom, often using stubs for lower levels.

   - Bottom-Up: Start integration from the lower-level modules, using drivers for higher-level modules.

   - Sandwich/Hybrid: Incorporates both top-down and bottom-up approaches.

4. Execute Tests: Run test cases to validate interactions and data flow.

5. Analyse Results: Investigate failures, debug issues, and fix defects.

6. Regression Testing: Ensure no new issues arise from the fixes.

Benefits

- Improved Quality: Increases the reliability of the system by ensuring components work together.

- Risk Reduction: Identifies potential issues before customer deployment.

- Cost Efficiency: Reduces downstream costs by catching errors early.

Challenges

- Complexity: Managing the intricacies involved in integrating various system parts.

- Time Constraints: Requires meticulous planning and execution, which can be time-consuming.

- Tool Selection: Choosing the appropriate tools and techniques for effective testing can be challenging.

Conclusion

System integration testing is vital for delivering a functioning, cohesive, and high-quality system. Proper planning, execution, and adoption of suitable methodologies and tools ensure the effective discovery and resolution of integration issues.

Acceptance Testing

Acceptance testing is a critical phase in the software development lifecycle. It ensures that the system meets business needs and requirements before going live. Here's a quick rundown:

Purpose

- Validation: Ensure the system meets the agreed-upon requirements and specifications.

- User Acceptance: Provide stakeholders and end-users with the opportunity to validate the solution and approve its readiness for use.

- Risk Mitigation: Identify issues that may impact the user's experience or business operations.

Types of Acceptance Testing

1. User Acceptance Testing (UAT): Conducted by end-users to validate the functionality and performance in real-world scenarios.

2. Business Acceptance Testing (BAT): Ensures that the software aligns with business objectives and processes.

3. Regulatory Acceptance Testing: Verifies that the software complies with relevant laws and regulations.

4. Operational Acceptance Testing (OAT): Tests operational readiness, including backup, recovery, maintenance, and security.

Key Activities

1. Planning: Define test objectives, scope, and criteria for acceptance.

2. Design Test Cases: Create test scenarios that reflect real-world use cases and activities.

3. Environment Setup: Prepare a test environment that simulates the production setting.

4. Execution: Run the test cases with active participation from the end-users or stakeholders.

5. Feedback Collection: Gather feedback from end-users to identify any discrepancies or unmet needs.

6. Issue Resolution: Address and resolve any defects or issues identified during testing.

Benefits

- Building Confidence: Ensures stakeholders that the system meets expectations and functions as required.

- Improved Quality: Identifies areas of improvement before release, leading to better user satisfaction.

- Preventative: Reduces the likelihood of post-deployment issues or rework.

Challenges

- User Buy-in: Ensuring active participation and commitment from end-users can be challenging.

- Defining Clear Criteria: Establishing unequivocal acceptance criteria is crucial yet difficult.

- Time Constraints: Completing comprehensive testing within limited timeframes can be difficult.

Conclusion

Acceptance testing is essential for validating the system's readiness for production deployment. It bridges the gap between development and operational use, ensuring that the software aligns with user expectations and business requirements. Proper planning, execution, and collaboration with stakeholders lead to successful acceptance testing and ultimately, satisfactory software delivery.

Seven Testing Principles

Testing shows the presence of defects, not their absence

That's a great point! The saying "Testing shows the presence of defects, not their absence" highlights a fundamental truth in software testing. Here's a bit more about it:

Understanding the Statement

- Purpose of Testing: Testing is primarily conducted to find defects or bugs in the software. When a defect is found, it confirms the presence of an issue that needs resolution.

- Limit of Testing: No matter how extensive or thorough the testing is, it's impossible to guarantee that a software product is completely free of defects.

- Risk Reduction: Testing significantly reduces the risk of defects in production but cannot eliminate the risk entirely.

Implications

- Continuous Improvement: Always aim for ongoing testing and improvement. The goal is to minimise defects, not eliminate them altogether.

- Comprehensive Coverage: While 100% coverage is often unattainable, diversifying test cases and exploring different scenarios can help uncover more defects.

- Feedback Loop: Use testing as a means to learn and iterate on the software development process rather than the end goal itself.

- Quality Assurance as a Process: Quality assurance isn't just about finding defects but also about improving processes to prevent future defects.

Practical Application

- Incremental Testing: Regular, iterative testing can help catch defects early and manage them effectively.

- Automated Testing: Utilise automated tests for repetitive and critical areas but complement them with manual testing for exploratory purposes.

- Collaboration: Involve developers, QA professionals, and stakeholders in the testing process for diverse perspectives and thorough validation.

Conclusion

Testing is a tool for identifying defects and improving quality, but it shouldn't be relied upon to prove perfection. Embrace it as part of a larger strategy to build reliable, user-friendly software.

Exhaustive testing is impossible

Absolutely, the idea that "exhaustive testing is impossible" is another core concept in software testing and engineering. Here's what it encompasses:

Explanation

- Infinite Input Combinations: In most software applications, the number of possible input combinations and execution paths is virtually infinite, making it impractical to test every single one.

- Complex Systems: Modern software systems often interact with various external systems and components, adding to the complexity and potential test cases.

- Time and Resource Constraints: Organisations don't have unlimited time or resources, making it necessary to prioritise testing efforts rather than attempting to test everything exhaustively.

Implications

- Risk-Based Testing: Focus on testing the most critical parts of the application where defects could have the greatest impact.

- Prioritisation: Prioritise test cases based on factors such as user impact, frequency of use, and past defect history.

- Balancing Act: Strive for a balance between automated and manual testing to optimally cover significant areas without aiming for 100% completeness.

Best Practices

- Identify Critical Paths: Focus on high-risk areas and critical business functionalities that power core aspects of the application.

- Use of Heuristics: Employ heuristics and risk analysis to predict where defects are more likely to appear based on similar past experiences.

- Test Plans and Strategies: Develop comprehensive test strategies and plans to cover high-priority features, leaving room for exploratory testing.

Conclusion

Exhaustive testing being impossible is a reminder to adopt a strategic, efficient, and thoughtful approach to testing. It emphasises the importance of smart testing over trying to cover every possible scenario, ensuring that testing efforts are focused where they are most needed.

Early testing saves time and money

Definitely! Early testing in the software development lifecycle is a practice that can lead to significant savings in both time and money. Here's how it works and why it's beneficial:

Explanation

- Early Bug Detection: Finding and fixing bugs early in the development process is much cheaper and easier than discovering them later. The cost of fixing a defect increases exponentially the later it is found.

- Shift-Left Testing: Implementing testing processes early in development—often referred to as "shifting left"—helps in identifying issues at the requirement or design phase rather than during or after development.

Benefits

- Cost Savings: Addressing issues early reduces the risk of larger-scale problems that could arise later, cutting down on expensive rework and patching.

- Time Efficiency: Early detection can lead to faster delivery of high-quality software, as less time is wasted on troubleshooting and fixing defects after the code is written.

- Improved Quality: Early and continuous testing leads to improved software quality, as it ensures that defects are caught at a stage where understanding the context and cause is easier.

Strategies

- Integrate Testing in Development: Make testing an integral part of the development process so that issues can be identified as code is written.

- Use Automated Testing: Implement automated testing tools to quickly check code against expected functionality right from the start.

- Adopt Continuous Integration: Utilise continuous integration practices to continuously test new code changes, ensuring quality and functionality are maintained.

Conclusion

Early testing acts as a preventative measure, helping to ensure that the software development process is streamlined, more predictable, and less prone to spiralling costs and time delays due to undetected errors. By catching issues before they escalate, early testing contributes to smoother operations and a more robust product.

Defects cluster together

Absolutely! The phenomenon that defects tend to cluster together is a well-documented observation in software development and is often referred to as the "defect cluster" phenomenon. Here's a deeper look at this concept:

Explanation

- Defect Clustering Principle: This principle, also known as the "80/20 rule" or Pareto principle in software testing, suggests that 80% of the defects are usually found in 20% of the modules.

Reasons for Clustering

1. Complex Code: More complex modules or functions in a codebase often lead to more defects. Complexity can arise from intricate logic, numerous dependencies, or a lack of clear documentation.

2. High Change Volume: Modules that undergo frequent changes are more prone to defects. Each change introduces a risk of introducing new errors if not managed carefully.

3. Developer Familiarity: Code written in a rush or by less experienced developers might have more defects due to oversight or lack of expertise.

4. Neglected Code: Parts of the code that are rarely revisited might have hidden defects, especially if they haven't been updated or reviewed often.

5. Inadequate Testing: Some sections of code may be under-tested due to lack of test coverage, leading to undetected defects.

Strategies to Address Defect Clustering

- Focused Testing: Allocate more testing resources to the modules known for defect clustering by using risk-based testing approaches.

- Code Reviews and Refactoring: Regular code reviews and refactoring can help identify and rectify problematic patterns that may lead to defects.

- Metrics and Monitoring: Use software metrics to identify areas of the code that correlate with high defect rates and focus on improving those areas.

- Improve Team Skills: Provide training and resources to improve the team's ability to handle complex code and reduce the chance of defects.

Conclusion

Understanding and addressing defect clustering is essential for improving software quality. By focusing on areas known to have high defect rates and employing strategies to manage and reduce these issues, teams can create more reliable and efficient software. Additionally, leveraging historical data and metrics can guide better planning and resource allocation, ensuring comprehensive coverage of potentially problematic areas.

Pesticide Paradox - Tests wear out

The "Pesticide Paradox" is a concept from software testing that refers to the diminishing effectiveness of tests over time if they remain unchanged. Here's a detailed breakdown of this paradox:

Explanation of the Pesticide Paradox

- Analogy: The term is borrowed from agriculture, where insects develop resistance to a particular pesticide over time. Similarly, in software testing, the same set of tests, if repeated constantly, lose their effectiveness in detecting new defects.

Why Tests Wear Out

1. Code Changes: Software evolves, and as such, the same test cases might no longer be relevant or adequate to catch new issues that arise from code changes.

2. Defect Immunisation: Existing defects identified by current test cases will be fixed, and the tests will then consistently pass. Without updates, they fail to catch new, subtle defects.

3. Adaptation: Developers might unconsciously start building to the test, which means they ensure the code passes the tests without necessarily focusing on overall code quality.

4. Context Loss: Over time, as the application and its requirements evolve, tests may not align with the current business context or user behaviours.

Strategies to Combat the Pesticide Paradox

1. Test Case Review and Refresh: Regularly review and update test cases, ensuring they are relevant and effective against the latest version of the software.

2. Test Automation Updates: Continuously update test automation scripts to adapt to changes in the application, environment, and user interactions.

3. Randomised and Exploratory Testing: Incorporate different testing techniques like exploratory testing to uncover defects not addressed by automated or regression tests.

4. Risk-Based Testing: Focus on areas of the application that are more prone to defects or have undergone significant changes.

5. Continuous Learning and Improvement: Encourage a learning environment where testers are continuously improving their skills and techniques to adapt better and enhance test coverage.

Conclusion

To maintain the effectiveness of testing processes and ensure they continue to add value, it's crucial to recognise the Pesticide Paradox. By diversifying testing strategies, regularly refreshing test cases, and being adaptive to changes, teams can enhance their ability to detect defects and improve software quality. This proactive approach ensures that testing remains a crucial and effective component in the software development lifecycle.

Testing is context dependent

The idea that "Testing is context dependent" is a fundamental principle in software testing, emphasising that the effectiveness and appropriateness of testing strategies and techniques are heavily influenced by the specific context in which they are applied. Here's a closer look at this concept:

Key Aspects of Context-Dependent Testing

1. Project Goals and Requirements:

   - Every project has unique goals, objectives, and requirements. The testing approach should align with these to ensure that the right aspects of the software are validated.

2. Type of Application:

   - Different types of applications (web, mobile, desktop, embedded systems) have unique characteristics, requiring specialised testing approaches.

3. Industry Standards:

 - Different industries (e.g., healthcare, finance, gaming) may have specific regulations, compliance requirements, or quality standards that dictate the testing approach.

4. Risk Assessment:

 - The level of risk involved in certain areas of the application influences how testing is prioritised. High-risk areas may need more thorough and extensive testing.

5. Technology and Tools:

 - The technology stack and tools available can determine the best ways to test the application. For instance, specific tools may be better suited to certain types of testing like performance, security, or usability.

6. Team Skills and Expertise:

- The skills and experience of the testing team can also impact the choice of testing techniques. Teams may favour approaches that align with their expertise.

7. Budget and Time Constraints:

- Limited resources and strict deadlines can affect the scope and depth of testing. Decisions might need to be made to prioritise certain tests over others.

8. User Expectations:

- Understanding the end-users and their expectations can guide testing to ensure that the software meets user needs and provides a good user experience.

Why Context Matters

- Efficiency: Context-appropriate testing ensures that efforts are focused on the most critical aspects of the application, optimising the use of resources.

- Effectiveness: Tailoring testing to the specific context increases the likelihood of uncovering meaningful defects and contributing to software quality.

- Flexibility: A context-driven approach allows for adjustments in testing strategy as the project evolves.

Conclusion

Context in software testing provides the foundation for making informed, pragmatic decisions about which testing strategies, tools, and techniques to employ. By recognising the unique circumstances of each project, testers can design and execute an effective testing process that addresses the relevant challenges and needs, delivering software that meets both technical standards and user expectations.

Absence-of-errors is a fallacy

The "absence-of-errors" fallacy is indeed an interesting concept. It refers to the flawed notion that just because no errors or problems are currently visible, there must be no problems at all. This fallacy can lead to complacency and a false sense of security in various fields like software development, quality assurance, and even in arguments.

Here's a deeper dive into this concept:

1. False Security: Believing everything is perfect just because issues haven't surfaced yet can lead to neglect in checking systems, processes, or arguments for potential flaws.

2. Importance in Software: In software development, just because a system isn't showing bugs doesn't mean it's flawless. There may be latent bugs waiting to emerge under certain conditions or usage patterns.

3. Human Reasoning: In logical reasoning, someone might conclude that since no one has proven their argument wrong, it must be right. This is a fallacy because absence of evidence is not evidence of absence.

4. Quality Assurance: Regular testing and examination are vital, as most errors tend to show up under specific circumstances or after a certain period, revealing issues that might have been overlooked.

5. Proactive Measures: Systems, whether mechanical, digital, or theoretical, should have proactive checks to uncover hidden issues before they escalate into significant problems.

By understanding the "absence-of-errors" fallacy, we can develop more resilient systems and strengthen arguments by actively seeking potential weaknesses rather than presuming they don't exist

Summary

This book provides a comprehensive overview of key aspects of software testing. It's structured around four core themes: Test Activities and Tasks, Test Types, Test Levels, and Seven Testing Principles.

Test Activities and Tasks:

The book begins by laying out the foundational activities and tasks that testers perform throughout the software development lifecycle. It covers test planning, design, execution, and reporting, offering practical insights and examples to help testers collaborate effectively with development teams and stakeholders.

Test Types:

Understanding the variety of test types is essential for a comprehensive testing approach. This section explores functional, non-functional, regression, and acceptance testing, among others. It guides the reader in selecting the right test types according to project goals and requirements, ensuring thorough evaluation of the software's functionality and performance.

Test Levels:

In this part, the book breaks down different levels of testing, including unit, system, and integration tests. Each level is explained in terms of objectives, benefits, and methodologies, helping readers stack and execute these levels to create a robust framework that enhances software quality.

Seven Testing Principles:

Drawing wisdom from industry experience, the book discusses seven testing principles: testing shows the presence of defects, exhaustive testing is impossible, early testing, defect clustering, the pesticide paradox, testing is context-dependent, and absence-of-errors fallacy. These principles guide readers in crafting thoughtful and efficient testing strategies.

Together, these sections provide a solid foundation for understanding and mastering software testing, making this book an essential resource for both newcomers and experienced practitioners seeking to enhance their testing skills and contribute effectively to software development projects.

The Art of Software Testing

 Foundations of Scrum Agile
Education

£2.99

App Store

Google Play

The Art of Software Testing

Agile Development with DevOps

Agile Project Management: Navigating Pros and Cons of Scrum, Kanban and combining them

Agile Tales

Air Traffic Control & Baggage Handling: A Kanban Story

Boundary Value Analysis

Communication Troubles of a Scrum Team

Disney's FastPass: A Queue Story

Henry Ford Assembly Line

Imperative of Software Testing: The Post Office Horizon Scandal

Introducing the Douglass Model for Agile Coaches

Kaizen: The Philosophy of Continuous Improvement for Business and Education

Mastering Software Quality Assurance: A Comprehensive Guide

McDonald's: A Kanban Story

Nightclub Entry Token System: A Kanban Story

Pizza Delivery: A Kanban Story

Scrum: Unveiling the Agile Method

The Art of Software Testing

Testing SaaS: A Comprehensive Guide to Software Testing for Cloud-Based Applications

The Agile Way to Fitness: Achieving fitness goals for IT professionals

The Art of Lean: Production Systems and Marketing Strategies in the modern era

The Art of Software Testing

The Art of Waterfall: A Traditional Approach to Project Management

The Board: A day-to-day feel of life on a Kanban team

The Sprint: A day-to-day feel of life on a Scrum team

The Whole Game: Systems Thinking Approach to Invasion Sports

Traffic Light System: A Kanban Story

V-Model

Zara's Just-In-Time (JIT) Model

www.ingramcontent.com/pod-product-compliance
Lightning Source LLC
LaVergne TN
LVHW012337060326
832902LV00012B/1912